First published in 2025 by

Melbourne, Australia
wdog.com.au

ISBN: 978-1-74203-709-7

10 9 8 7 6 5 4 3 2 1 25 26 27 28 29

Printed and bound in China by Everbest Printing Investment Limited

Wild Dog would like to thank Graham Moore and Jeni Kalowsky from the Entomological Society of Victoria for their careful fact checking.

A catalogue record for this book is available from the National Library of Australia

FSC® is a non-profit international organisation established to promote the responsible management of the world's forests.

Image Credits: front cover CHAINFOTO24; pp2–3 aerogondo2; pp4–5 Natalia van D; pp6–7 Noradoa; p7 (inset, top right) CHAINFOTO24, p7 (inset, bottom) puyalroyo; p7 (inset, top left) AbuMazna; pp8–9 Cornel Constantin; pp10–11 Darkdiamond67; p10 (inset, top left) Breck P. Kent; p10 (inset, right) Kalebjeppson125; pp12–13 jakrit yuenprakhon; p13 (inset, left) Sari ONeal; p13 (inset, right) Holger Kirk; p13 (inset, bottom) Christian Vinces; pp14–15 Brian Woolman; p14 (inset, top left) Rasmuscool99; p15 (inset) Ciungara; p16 Leena Robinson; p17 (inset, top) Cathy Keifer; p17 (inset, bottom) Cathy Keifer; pp18–19 24Novembers; p18 (inset, bottom) Johan Larson; p19 (inset, top left) John A. Anderson; p19 (inset, bottom right) ATOM WANG; pp20–21 Pone, p20 (inset, bottom left) Pong Wira; p20 (inset, bottom right) Butterfly Hunter; p21 (inset) Aperna K Mohan; pp22–23 Jeremy Wee; p23 (inset) jakrit yuenprakhon; pp24–25 AbuMazna; p24 (inset) Ken Griffiths; pp26–27 Ansis Klucis; pp28–29 Isabelle Ohara; pp30–31 aerogondo2; back cover (top left) Cathy Keifer

UP CLOSE

MARK RUSSELL

Butterflies

Butterflies are insects. There are more than 15,000 species of butterfly in the world. At least 400 species are found in Australia.

You might have seen:

THE MONARCH BUTTERFLY

THE CABBAGE WHITE BUTTERFLY

THE ULYSSES BUTTERFLY

Butterflies are a species of **LEPIDOPTERA**, a group which also includes moths and skippers.

Lepidoptera means 'scale wing' in Ancient Greek. Butterfly wings are covered in scales so delicate they will brush off if touched.

Butterflies **METAMORPHOSE**, which means they take different physical forms throughout their life cycle. There are four stages to a butterfly's life: egg, larva, pupa and adult.

1. Egg

2. Larva (caterpillar)

4. Adult
3. Pupa (chrysalis)

Most female butterflies lay their **EGGS** on the leaves of a specific host plant. This is the plant that its caterpillars will prefer to eat.

Some species of butterfly lay eggs one at a time. Others lay small groups of eggs. Some can lay hundreds at a time.

Butterfly eggs have a protective outer layer of shell called the **CHORION**. Inside that shell there is a thin layer of wax to stop the egg from drying out.

Butterfly larvae are called **CATERPILLARS**. Caterpillars spend their whole lives eating — they can eat up to four times their own body weight every day and grow up to 100 times their size over a few weeks.

They mostly feed on plants, but some eat other insects.

The first thing the caterpillar eats is its own eggshell!

Caterpillars have extra legs called **PROLEGS**. Prolegs can help the caterpillar grip to surfaces, but because they have no joints or segments, they are not real legs! So even though it doesn't look like it, a caterpillar only has six legs!

When it is fully grown, the caterpillar finds a safe place to undergo its metamorphosis — usually hanging beneath a leaf or branch.

The caterpillar fastens itself to the underside of the leaf with a silk button which it produces itself.

The caterpillar sheds its skin, revealing the **CHRYSALIS** underneath.

Inside the chrysalis, the caterpillar is liquified and reassembled as a butterfly.

When the butterfly is fully grown it emerges from its chrysalis. It has four wings, six legs, two antennae, and an external shell called an EXOSKELETON that protects its organs.

The butterfly hangs from the case while its wings dry out. After an hour or so it will be able to fly.

On the top of the butterfly's head are two **ANTENNAE**. Antennae are used to detect smells and motion. They can also help with balance.

Butterflies breath through tiny holes in their abdomens. These are called **SPIRACLES**.

Their **COMPOUND** eyes are made up of many smaller lenses – up to 17,000 in each eye. Unlike humans, butterflies can see backwards, forwards, above and below at the same time. They can also see ultraviolet light.

The butterfly uses its **PROBOSCIS** like a straw to suck up liquids. Most feed on things like flower nectar, fruit juices and sap.

The lifespan of a butterfly varies. The Monarch Butterfly lives up to eight months, while the Cabbage White Butterfly only lives about three weeks.

PREDATORS such as spiders, wasps and birds eat butterflies.

Some butterflies **CAMOUFLAGE** themselves to blend with their surroundings. Others have markings that look like eyes to scare away predators, or bright colours that indicate that they are poisonous.

Butterflies attract mates using bright colours and patterns, or by releasing smells called PHEROMONES from special scales on their wings or structures on their abdomens. Others create sounds by rubbing or clicking their legs or wings, or go on courtship flights.

Butterflies mate by joining their abdomens together. The male passes sperm to the female to **FERTILISE** her eggs.

Butterfly or Moth?

Can you tell the difference? While there are some exceptions, in general:

- Butterflies are active during the day while moths are active at night.
- Butterflies are usually brightly coloured while moths are duller.
- Butterflies rest with their wings held vertically while moths rest with their wings held horizontally.
- Moths have feathery antennae.
- A moth pupa spins a cocoon, while a butterfly's chrysalis is a layer of hardened skin.

Fossils of butterflies show they have been on earth for almost 200 million years. Butterflies feature in Australian Aboriginal Dreaming stories, and often symbolise transformation and life cycles.

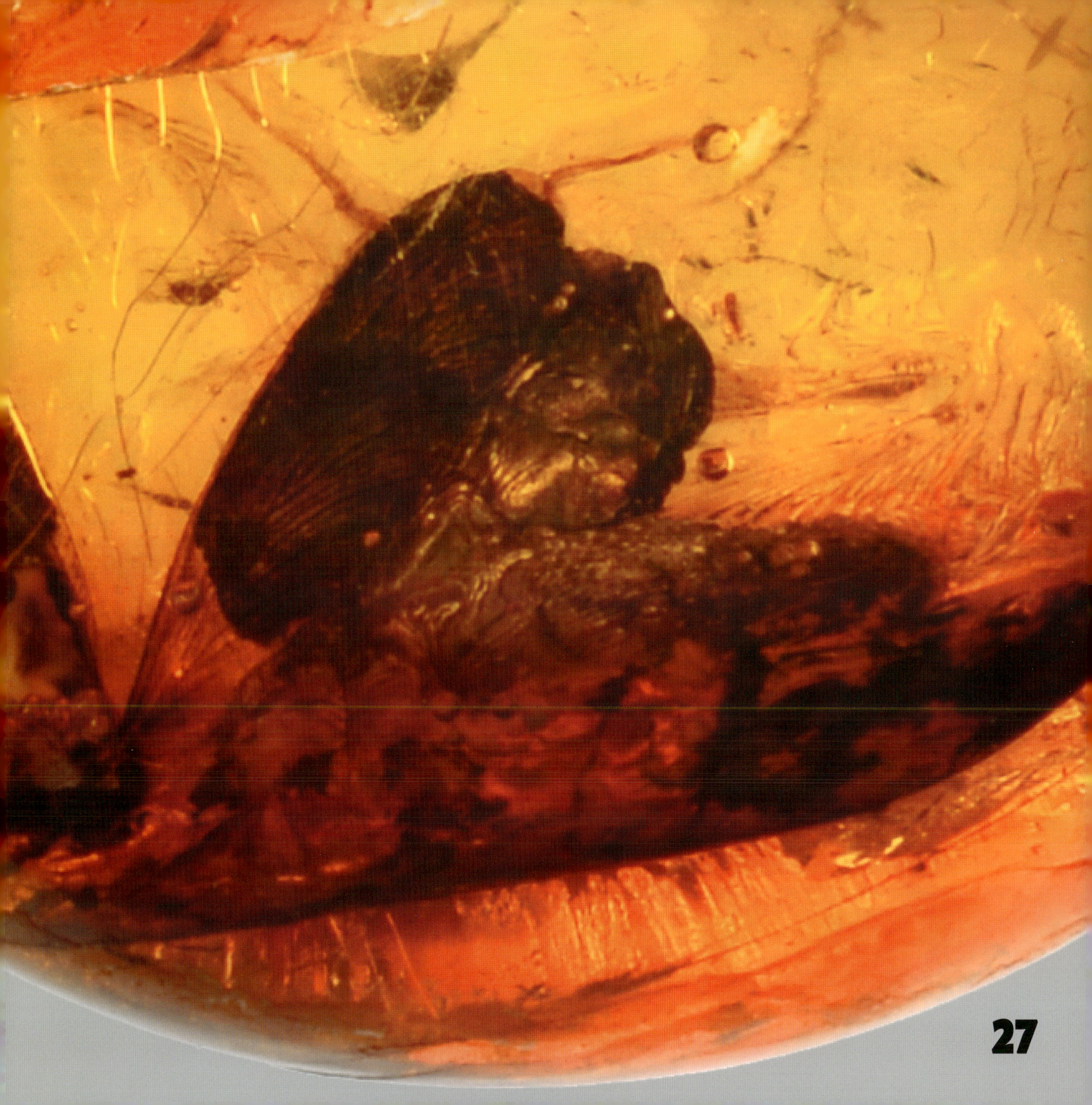

Glossary

Abdomen: the main section of the body

Chorion: the outermost shell around an insect egg

Chrysalis: the pupal stage of the butterfly, enclosed in a sealed skin

Compound Eye: an eye made up of many smaller lenses

Egg: a capsule containing the reproductive cells and nutrients

Exoskeleton: a rigid shell that protects the soft tissues of certain animals

Fertilise: the fusion of hereditary material from two different cells

Fossil: the remains or impression of a plant or animal embedded in rock and preserved

Host Plants: the plant on which a butterfly lays its eggs. The caterpillar eats this plant when it hatches

Larva: the life cycle stage after hatching but before reaching adulthood

Metamorphosis: a significant change in an animal's physical form after birth, which also affects behaviour

Pheromone: a chemical secreted by an organism that affects other members of its species

Predator: an animal that hunts other species for food

Proboscis: the elongated appendage from the head of a butterfly, used as a straw to suck up liquids

Pupa: the life cycle stage during which the larva breaks down and metamorphoses into an adult

Proleg: fleshy appendages not considered true legs

Species: a population of living things capable of reproducing

Spiracles: breathing holes in the butterfly's abdomen